Dealing with BULLIES

Written by Cristie Reed

Content Consultant
Taylor K. Barton, LPC
School Counselor

Rourke
Educational Media

rourkeeducationalmedia.com

Scan for Related Titles
and Teacher Resources

www.rourkeeducationalmedia.com

PHOTO CREDITS: Cover: © MBI_Images; page 4: © Dawn Lackner; page 5: © Steve Debenport (top), © kristian sekulic (bottom); page 6: © Christopher O Driscoll; pages 7, 9, 14: © fstop123; pages 10, 15: © Svetlana Braun; page 11: © Tracy Whiteside; page 13: © Patrick Herrera; page 16: © manley099; page 17: © Steve Debenport; page 18: © Rudyanto Wijaya; page 20: © kali9; page 21: © Rmarmion; page 22: © GlobalStock

Edited by Precious McKenzie

Cover and Interior Design by Tara Raymo

Library of Congress PCN Data

Dealing with Bullies / Cristie Reed
(Social Skills)
ISBN 978-1-62169-906-4 (hard cover) (alk. paper)
ISBN 978-1-62169-801-2 (soft cover)
ISBN 978-1-62717-012-3 (e-Book)
Library of Congress Control Number: 2013937301

Rourke Educational Media
Printed in the United States of America,
North Mankato, Minnesota

Also Available as:

ROURKE'S e-Books

Rourke Educational Media

rourkeeducationalmedia.com

customersevice@rourkeeducationalmedia.com • PO Box 643328 Vero Beach, Florida 32964

TABLE OF CONTENTS

WHAT IS BULLYING?

A fifth grade girl spreads mean stories about another girl in her class. Every morning on the way to school, a group of bigger boys kick and shove a smaller boy. Every day, a fourth grade girl receives cruel text messages from another girl at her school. All of these situations are examples of bullying.

Bullying happens when someone tries to harm someone else. Hitting, kicking, and shoving are **physical** bullying. Name-calling, cruel words, or threats are **verbal** bullying. Bullying is intentional. A bully is someone that purposefully **torments** others over and over again.

FACTS ABOUT BULLYING

Bullying can happen anywhere. But, most of the time, bullying happens at school, in the hallways, the classroom, at lunch, and on the playground. Anyone can be a bully, boys, girls, big kids, or small kids. Bullying occurs face-to-face and also takes place through text messages, phone calls, and emails. When bullying occurs over the Internet or with cell phones it is called **cyber-bullying**.

STOP CYBER-BULLYING

1. Don't respond to bullying messages online or on the phone.
2. Talk to an adult about bullying messages.
3. Block the person that sends bullying messages.
4. Never share personal information about yourself or others online.
5. Ask an adult to show you how to be safe online.

Bullying involves the bully, the person being bullied, and the people who see it happen, or the **bystanders**. All three suffer when bullying takes place. Bullying can start with hurtful teasing. Extreme bullying rises to property damage and serious physical and **mental** harm.

Bystanders often feel helpless and guilty.

They struggle with whether or not to report the incident.

BULLYING HURTS

Bullying is serious. Bullying causes **emotional** damage that can last for many years. Bullying makes people feel nervous, worried, and scared. It can cause people to lose sleep and not eat. If bullying goes on for a long time, it can cause serious health problems. When someone is being bullied, they may start to become **depressed** and avoid everyday activities. Their school performance may go down. Victims of bullying become sad, lonely, and may even start acting out.

Warning Signs

- Losing interest in school work or favorite activities
- Not wanting to go to school
- Not feeling well
- Falling grades
- Avoiding situations with peers
- Feeling sad, lonely, depressed, or angry
- Loss of self-esteem
- Acting out in unusual ways, such as fighting
- Torn clothes or unexplained injuries
- Losing important items

WHY DO SOME KIDS BULLY?

Some kids want to hurt others to make themselves feel more important. They want to feel more popular with their peers. They believe that hurting others will help them gain status with their group of friends. Other bullies may need to feel in control. Some bullies have been tormented themselves. They bully others to feel better about themselves.

Bullies need a victim. They target someone who seems physically weaker than themselves. They may look for someone who is smaller in size or younger in age. But, victims aren't always smaller in stature. Bullies also look for emotional weakness in others. They target victims who lack confidence or seem timid.

Bullies are a lot like predators in the animal kingdom.

They look for weak individuals and then attack.

DEALING WITH TOUGH SITUATIONS

Talking to an older brother or sister can help.
They may have faced bullying in the past.

Bullies don't expect you to stand up to them. But you can stand up to bullies and stop their mean behavior. You don't have to do it alone. Get help from friends, parents, and your school. Everyone needs to work together when bullying happens.

There are several steps to take if you are faced with bullying.

- Try to stay calm.
- You can tell the bully to stop.
- You can try to act brave and walk away.
- You can try to act like you don't care.
- Avoid the bully.
- Don't be alone. Stay with groups of friends.
- Don't try to deal with the bully by yourself.
- Don't fight back.
- Don't respond to the bully with yelling or screaming.
- Don't try to solve the problem by bullying back.
- If you are bullied or see bullying happen, get help.
- Tell someone that you trust. Talk to a friend, a parent, or a teacher.
- Work together to find the best solution for the problem.

These may be hard steps to take. But it is important to try to solve the problem and end the bullying before it goes too far.

If you are ever faced with a bullying situation, remember that it's not your fault. You are not alone. Bullying happens to all kinds of people in all kinds of places. If you are ever the victim or a bystander, get help so that you can act in a responsible way.

Set an example for fair treatment of others.
Let people know you have zero tolerance for bullies.
By standing up to bullying, you become
an upstander instead of a bystander.

CHOOSE KINDNESS

At some time in their life, most kids will say or do something to hurt another person. It's part of growing up. A person may be mean or hurtful, just by accident. However, most people learn from their mistakes. Most people don't continue to hurt others intentionally. That's what makes bullying different. A bully doesn't show **empathy** for others. Their cruel behavior is meant to hurt again and again.

It is important to learn to treat other people with **dignity**. Be aware of how your words and actions affect others. It is important to be a good friend and show kindness to everyone.

GLOSSARY

bystanders (BYE-stan-durz): people who are at a place when something happens to someone else

cyber-bullying (SYE-bur-BUL-ee-ing): bullying that occurs through cell phones or over the Internet

depressed (di-PREST): feeling sad or gloomy

dignity (DIG-nuh-tee): a quality or manner that makes a person worthy of honor or respect

emotional (e-MOH-shuh-nuhl): to do with your feelings

empathy (EM-puh-thee): understanding the feelings of others

mental (MEN-tuhl): to do with or done by the mind

physical (FIZ-uh-kuhl): to do with the body

torments (tor-MENTS): upsets or annoys someone deliberately

verbal (VUR-buhl): to do with words

INDEX

WEBSITES TO VISIT

www.stopbullying.gov/kids

www.kidsturncentral.com/links/bullylinks.htm

www.pbskids.org/itsmylife/friends/bullies

ABOUT THE AUTHOR

Cristie Reed lives in Florida with her husband and her dog, Rocky. She has been a teacher and reading specialist for 32 years. She hopes all children love to read. She believes that reading can help people overcome any problem, even a problem as serious as bullying.

Meet The Author!
www.meetREMauthors.com